Are You Crazy?

A Good Look at Jeff and Louise

Jeffrey D. Johnson

Wipf & Stock
PUBLISHERS
Eugene, Oregon

Wipf and Stock Publishers
199 W 8th Ave, Suite 3
Eugene, OR 97401

Are You Crazy?
A Good Look at Jeff and Louise
By Johnson, Jeffrey D.

ISBN 13: 978-1-55635-079-5
ISBN 10: 1-55635-079-1
Publication date 11/30/2006

About Israel Today Ministries

Three-fold Purpose:

- Teach the Church about Israel
- Teach Israel about their Messiah
- Help feed those in need (Romans 15:27; Genesis 12:1-3)

To receive Dr. Johnson's "teaching letters," or, if you would like to send a gift to Israel Today Ministries, or if you would like Dr. Johnson to speak at your church event, school, or small group, contact:

Israel Today Ministries
P.O. Box 150288
Arlington, TX 76015
Phone/Fax 817.468.4441
E mail: Galileeman@juno.com

This is Yossef (Joseph) and Abigail. Your monthly donations help feed little ones like these.

"Inasmuch as ye have done it unto one of the least of these my brethren, ye have done it unto me" –Jesus, Matthew 25:40

About Dr. Jeffrey D. Johnson

- Three decades in ministry
- Founder/Director of Israel Today Ministries
- Director of tours to the Middle East
- Senior pastor in Ohio, Massachusetts and California
- Almost 7 years directorship with International Ministries to Israel (formerly, The American Association for Jewish Evangelism, where the famed Hyman Appelman was the first president)
- Conference speaker
- Bible expositor
- Guest lecturer
- Author

Born and raised in the Midwest, Dr. Johnson took his B.D. from Massillon Baptist College, his MA from Moody Bible Institute, and his Th.M. and Th.D. from Christian Bible College. His passion for Israel, the Jewish roots of Christianity and Bible prophecy, is well known. His teaching will stir your heart to follow the Lord and to love and *"pray for the peace of Jerusalem"* (Psalm 122:6).

As an "Itinerant Bible Teacher," Dr. Johnson will travel anywhere to proclaim God's redeeming Grace through our Lord and Savior Jesus the Messiah, *"to the Jew first, and also to the Greek"* (Romans 1:16).

His call is to *"Teach the Church about Israel; Teach Israel about their Messiah; and to feed those in need"* (Genesis 12:3; Romans 15:27).

Dr. Jeff and his wife, Louise, have purposed to serve the Lord trusting God to provide the funds and resources for their livelihood.

Israel Today Ministries, founded by Dr. Johnson, is a faith ministry, supported by "love offerings" from those desiring to bless Israel. Dr. Jeff and Louise have been commissioned and sent out by their home church.

Comments from Christian Leaders

I am pleased to recommend him to churches as an able expositor of the Word of God.

– *the late* **John Walvoord**, Chancellor,
Dallas Theological Seminary

A Bible Expositor with special insights on the origin, nature and destiny of God's chosen people, Israel.

– **John C. Whitcomb**, Bible Scholar, Author, Professor

A careful expositor of Scripture.

– **Homer Kent**, President Emeritus,
Grace College and Seminary

A practitioner of all that he preaches.

– **Paige Patterson**, former President of the
Southern Baptist Convention, President,
Southeastern Baptist Theological Seminary

He has a wonderful grasp of Jewish history and liturgy.

– **Edgar C. James**, Professor, Moody Bible Institute

He is a person who has been uniquely prepared by God to preach and teach about God's special people. Any one who hears him will come away with a great love for the people of Abraham.

–**Dick Dahlquist**, Chair, Pastoral Studies, Acting Dean,
Grace College of Graduate Studies

He has a gifted teaching ministry which encompasses Biblical prophecy and insights into modern-day Judaism.

–the late **Paul Tassell**, Bible Scholar, Author,
former National Representative of the G.A.R.B.C.

He has a great ministry.

– **LaVerne Butler**, former President of Mid-Continent Baptist College, Scholar, Conference Speaker, President, Pulpit Aflame

Your heart will be thrilled as he ministers the prophetic Scriptures.

– the late **Alden A. Gannett**, President Emeritus of Southeastern Bible College, Bible Scholar, Author, Conference Speaker, President, Gannett Ministries

He loves the people and nation of Israel. He has given himself to a thorough study of God's ancient people and of the prophetic.

– **Ivan H. French**, Pastor Emeritus, Pleasant View Bible Church, former Professor, Grace College and Seminary

Table of Contents

Chapter 1
Are You Crazy?

I have been asked this question since I resigned the pastorate. On the one hand, humanly speaking, it doesn't make any sense to resign a very secure position where I was receiving a generous salary package with full benefits and perks.

Join me, as together we can follow the Lord on a journey that will take us to the regions beyond doing the impossible. "For with God nothing shall be impossible."

Resigning from being the senior pastor of a gracious and loving church wasn't an easy decision. Louise and I prayed for at least two years over this matter. Before, coming to the church as pastor I was the executive director of a Jewish mission in the Chicago area. One of the main founders of that mission was Hyman Appelman, the great Jewish evangelist of years past. I came to believe in Jesus under his ministry in 1973.

My love for Israel and Jewish people grew over the years and during my doctoral studies in the early 80's I developed a deep burden to help the church understand God's plan for Israel and Israel to understand more clearly about Jesus.

While in Chicago, Louise and I were in our niche as I spoke in churches, conferences, colleges and bible studies, and as she ran and organized the operations of the office and graced everyplace and everyone she touched.

Approximately seven years later, God directed us to a church that had experienced some difficult times. God used us to bring the church through the storm. The congregation loved us and was very generous in caring for Louise and me. However, our love for Israel simply intensified. After a few years God began once again to speak to our hearts and began to lead us in a direction that would necessitate an immeasurable amount of trusting in His provision.

What was this step of faith that God was showing us? It would mean that we would have to walk away from a secure and generous financial position with the church. It would mean starting something from scratch. "Wait a minute Lord! I am 47 years old and have great responsibilities and a respected position. I am securing plans for my future. Lord, surely you are not asking me to do this!"

What did He want me to do? Start a new mission outreach? Yes! Hold on, there are other good mission agencies out there in the f ield. Why a new one? Good question! What ingredients would make up this outreach?

This mission agency would have three main components:

1. Teach the church about Israel *(through sound bible teaching)*

2. Teach Israel about their Messiah *(through acts of charity and presenting the gospel)*

3. Help feed & clothe those in need *(to fulfill the mandate of Romans 15:17 & Genesis 12:1-3)*

Israel Today Ministries was born out of this crucible of prayer and passion for God's ancient people Israel and love for the church. Now it is beginning to make sense.

So, Louise and I have answered the call and literally stepped out in faith trusting completely in God's provision through people like you. Yes, humanly speaking this is crazy. However, knowing that this is God's leading in our lives, we must be obedient to Him. Therefore, it is the sanest thing we can do!

We trust the Lord to provide what is needed for our livelihood. This includes, medical, insurances, pension, taxes, housing etc. Each week we go to the mailbox to see what the Lord has provided.

The waves at times seem high, and yet, Jesus is just ahead of us.

We knew there would be a sacrifice and Louise and I are willing to march to the front of the line and offer ourselves unto the Lord. We also, know that God uses folks like you who give unto the Lord. You help underwrite Israel Today

Ministries. You gifts enables us to go and fulfill God's plan in blessing Abraham's seed.

Will you help us? Will you help Louise and me, and in so doing, bless Israel? If you already are standing with us through prayer and support, with all of our heart, we thank you.

Join Louise and me as we "teach the church about Israel" and "teach Israel about their Messiah" and "help feed & clothe those in need." Partner with us as together we can bless God's ancient people, Israel.

Are we crazy? No. We are simply following the Lord in a journey that is taking us to the regions beyond doing the impossible, and yet, it is not impossible, "for with God nothing shall be impossible."

Let us hear from you! Together we will bless Israel and touch the "Apple of God's eye."

Until He comes, we are
Together Under His Wings,
Jeff & Louise

Chapter 2
Our Debt

To say Christians owe a debt to the Jew is an understatement. The foundation upon which New Testament faith rests is the Hebrew Bible. The *"Tenach"*, or the Hebrew Bible (Old Testament), is comprised of three major divisions. *Torah* B the five books of Moses; *Nevi'im* B the Prophets and *Ketuvim* B the Writings.

All that Christians hold dear is derived from Judaism in some form. From the pews, altar, pulpit, baptism and officers of the church, including our reverence of the Scriptures stems from first century Judaism.

Jesus was Jewish. The Bible is a Jewish book written by Jewish writers (with one or two exceptions), about a Jewish Messiah who will bring redemption and a kingdom of universal peace. The Jewish apostles took the gospel to the Gentiles. Subsequently, all Gentiles who attend church on Sunday can thank the Jews for bringing them the message of Jesus the Messiah.

Believers owe a debt of gratitude and thanksgiving to the Jew. We can do this in part by learning about the Jewish culture, religion, and how to communicate the gospel message effectively and lovingly.

Both Jewish and Gentile People Need Jesus

Romans 1:16 states, *"For I am not ashamed of the gospel of Christ: for it is the power of God unto salvation to every one that believeth; to the Jew first, and also to the Greek."* Wherever Paul traveled he would address the Jews in that community first, then the Gentiles.

1. *Jewish people need Messiah.* All people, regardless of nationality or ethnic origin are under sin (Romans 3:9). There is not a separate method of salvation for the Jew. All people, both Jew and Gentile are guilty before God and are in need of redemption (Romans 3:19).

2. *Jesus commands us* to share the gospel with all people (Mark 16:15). Some Christians, even within the evangelical community, hold to a presupposition that the Jewish community has no need of hearing the gospel. And yet, Jesus commands us to go and communicate to both Jew and Gentile.

3. *The Apostle Paul reveals his burden* for the Jewish people in Romans chapters nine, ten and eleven. He expresses that having a concern for Israel's salvation is part of God's plan for the human race. He emphasized that God has not cast away His people. God loves them with an everlasting love. Paul also

enforced the reality that the Gentiles owe a great debt to the Jews. The non-Jew has been the recipient of the Word of God, the hope of Israel through the Messiah and eternal life with God because of the faithfulness of Jewish people taking the gospel to them. The great apostle stresses that there will be a day when Israel will become God's witnesses to the world, therefore, having a special place in God's program.

Blessings For Those Who Bless Israel

"And I will bless them tht bless thee, and curse him that curseth thee." Gen. 12:3

To discover the richness of the Jewish roots of Christianity and to touch the lives of Jewish people is to be richly blessed by God. God chose Israel simply because He loved her, *"For thou art an holy people unto the Lord thy God: the Lord thy God hath chosen thee to be a special people unto himself, above all people that are upon the face of the earth. The Lord did not set his love upon you, nor choose you, because ye were more in number than any people; for ye were the fewest of all people: but because the Lord loved you..."* Deut. 7:6-8

The blessing is six fold (Gen. 12:2,3):

1. *"I will make of thee a great nation."* Through Abraham came the Jewish nation. Also, through Abraham came a spiritual heritage to those of like faith. Plus, through Ishmael, came the Arab nations.

2. *"I will bless thee."* This was evident through the earthly blessings he received along the way. Plus, he was considered a *"friend of God"* (Jas 2:23).

3. *"And make thy name great."* Abraham's name is respected within the Jewish, Moslem and Christian communities. Along with the name of Christ, Abraham is one of the most widely known throughout the world.

4. *"And thou shalt be a blessing."* This expands throughout the world of both Jews and Gentiles. Abraham is an example of a man of great faith in God.

5. *"And I will bless them that bless thee, and curse him that curseth thee."* History verifies this statement. Those individuals and nations who helped Israel were blessed and those who stood against Israel were indeed cursed.

6. *"And in thee shall all the families of the earth be blessed."* This promise projects the coming of the Messiah from the seed of Abraham and considers all that Messiah is and will be. Below is a list of some of the messianic prophecies fulfilled in Jesus of Nazareth:

Messianic Prophecies

Prophecy	*OT Location*	*NT Fulfillment*
Seed of a woman	Gen. 3:15	1 Jn. 3:18;Gal. 4:4
Seed of Abraham	Gen. 12:3	Matt. 1:1
Tribe of Judah	Gen. 49:10	Heb.7:14;Matt. 1
Seed of David	Ps. 89:4; 132:11	Lk.1:22;Acts2:29

Born in Bethlehem	Micah 5:2	Matt. 2; Luke 2
Virgin Birth	Isa. 7:14	Matt. 1; Luke 1
Like Moses	Deut. 18:15,18	John 7; Acts 3
Triumphal Entry	Zech. 9:9	Matt. 21; John 12
Rejected	Isa. 53; Psa. 118	Jn. 1; Matt. 26
Betrayed	Psa. 41:9	Matt. 26; Mark 14
30 pieces of silver	Zech 11:12	Matt. 26
Forsaken	Zech. 13:7	Matt. 26
Condemned	Isa. 53:8	Matt. 27; Lk. 23
Silent	Isa. 53:7	Matt. 27; Lk. 23
Smitten, spat upon	Isa. 50:6; Mic. 5:1	Matt. 26; Lk. 22
Mocked	Psa. 22:7,8	Matt. 28:38-43
Crucifixion	Psa. 22:14,16,17	Matt. 27; Jn. 19
Suffer with transgressors	Isa. 53:12	Matt. 27; Lk. 23
Casting of Lots	Psa. 22:18	Matt. 27; Mk. 15
No broken bones	Exo. 12:46	John 19:31-36
Sacrificial Death	Isa. 53: 5-12	John 1;11; Acts 10
Rise Again	Psa. 16:10	Acts 2; Mark 16
At God's right hand	Psa. 110:1	Mark 16; Luke 24

Chapter 3
Climbing the Wall

A typical Israeli morning was unfolding as Louise and I were planning to go to Bethany the home of Mary and Martha and the place where Jesus raised Lazarus from the dead.

110 Degree Heat

Ramone was to be our guide. He is a trusted friend who watches over Louise and me, especially me, to keep us safe and out of trouble. In the past he waited three hours in the hot Jericho desert waiting for me and a dear friend to cross the boarder from Jordan. At that time my bag was stolen at the boarder. I asked Israeli soldiers for assistance. They promptly escorted me back to the Palestinian security area to look for my belongings. It was like the parting of the Red Sea. Once the Palestinian soldiers saw the five Israeli soldiers and this six foot two American they yielded and allowed me to look for my stuff. Unfortunately, we could not find my bag. Nevertheless, Ramone, did not know what was going on and faithfully waited in the 110 degree heat until I and my friend appeared. He was somewhat dehydrated, anxious and very relieved to see us. He was a sight to behold and I was thankful he stayed the course and waited for us in the desert sun. He is that kind of faithful brother.

Now back to the story. Ramone picked Louise and me up in which we made a few contacts and completed some busy work and then up to the Mount of Olives.

Blocked By the Wall

As you may know Israel is erecting a security fence around that will separated Israel from the future Palestine. The wall is not to keep people out, rather, to cause people to go through check points. This will aid Israel in stopping the bad guys from blowing up innocent bystanders shopping at the market or riding a bus.

The road leading to our destination ended up being blocked by the wall. This wall is around 25 feet tall and about 18 inches thick. We could either drive another hour and a half around the mountain and wall, or…

Where we were standing the wall ended, however, it was adjoined by another five foot wall making a T shape. This five foot wall went into the city of Bethany. The options were to climb over this five foot section or to drive around. Well you've guessed it. I looked at Louise and said, "Do you love me?" She said, "Let's do it!"

"Do You Love Me?"

Oh, did I tell you, there were Israeli soldiers guarding this section of the wall. We greeted the soldiers with a sheepish smile. Ramone was standing watch over the car. He said, "I will pray for you." That was somewhat comforting. Did I mention I am not 25 any more?? So, I began to climb the wall, holding on to the larger security wall so I would not fall backwards onto the sharp stones below. Standing on the top of the five foot wall, holding on to the large security wall, reaching my hand down to pull Louise up so she could stand on top of the smaller wall and hold on to the security wall while I stepped down on the other side. Then reaching up to grab her hand, Louise shimmied down and is now with me on the other side of the security fence, no longer under the protection of Israeli forces.

Hamas Representatives

We turned around only to be greeted by Hamas representatives with AK47 rifles. Fortunately, there was a barrage of press taking photos of us climbing over the wall. We swiftly passed through the soldiers and press to go on our way. Whew! By the way, if you see a photo on the internet of two people climbing over a wall in the Middle East, yes, it is really Louise and me.

We walked for some time through the village of Bethany until we found the tomb of Lazarus. The villagers were friendly and very helpful. Some were amazed that we were there walking through the streets. Being in the Holy Land is the ultimate contradiction. It is the most volatile chunk of real estate on the planet, and yet, it is the most peaceful, spiritually refreshing place to experience.

We literally journeyed down through a tunnel and crawled into the tomb and were silenced by the miracle that unfolded here two thousand years ago. To be reminded of the resurrection and assurance of eternal life in Christ Jesus was priceless. And yet, our hearts were reminded also of the millions of Jews and Arabs who do not know of God's redeeming grace through His son, the Lord Jesus.

Oh, by the way, we had to repeat the process to find our way back to Ramone, who once again was patiently waiting for his friends to return. As the sun was beginning to set, Louise and I were climbing back over the wall. Would we do it again? Yep!

Counting the Cost

To follow Jesus requires counting the cost. We all are on a journey. Whether we are patiently waiting, climbing, crawling or simply standing in silence. God provides what is needed at the exact moment. His grace is sufficient for today. He will also take care of tomorrow.

You see why your prayers, encouragement and financial support are greatly needed and appreciated. Thousands have been touched by our ministry in the Middle East. Together we are blessing the seed of Abraham.

God is in control of everything that takes place in our lives. His purpose will be fulfilled no matter how bleak it may look, no matter how challenging it may seem. *"Then Job answered the Lord and said: 'I know You can do everything, and that no purpose of Yours can be withheld from You"* (Job 42:1,2).

Thank you for your generous prayers, gifts and financial support. The need is great and the time is now.

"Time is short, life is precious and Jesus is coming soon!"

Chapter 4
The Phone Call

The streets were busy with the usual press of people selling their wares. It was afternoon, as my colleague and I were traveling in Jerusalem, when I received the phone call from one of my sons. Hearing your son's voice when you are in Israel and he is in another country within the Middle East is initially startling.

Scott and Jeff in Jordan.

This time he was in Jordan, which is a friendlier, pro-western Arab country in the region. Oftentimes, he is in another country nearby that is not so pro-western. Nevertheless, while in Jordan he was assisting a local congregation with some projects in a very poor section of the capital city Amman. During this time he became acquainted with a large Muslim family, a family of renown within their community. This dear family had shown my son gracious hospitality.

The head of the home is a distinguished gray haired businessman who is well respected in Amman. He has 4 sons and 5 daughters. He and his lovely wife are kind people living in a beautiful home within the upside of town.

Who is Your Father?

During this time my son was living in a lowly apartment near the projects of the poorest section of the capital city. However, this Muslim family invited my son to stay a few days. One of their daughters is a believer in Jesus which made the conversations very interesting. The father continued to ask my beloved son about his family. "Who is your father and what does he do?" "Where does your family live and where do they go?"

Family and reputation are very important in the Middle East. You are known by what you do and not so much by the words you speak, though your words are very important, rather, your actions speak volumes as to your character. Thus, the reason for the phone call from my son.

"Dad, can you come to Jordan and validate who I am?" he asked. I understood his request and the meaning behind it and I responded, "I will be there as soon as I can."

Our Plan

My colleague and I began making arrangements and preparations for our journey from Jerusalem to Amman. Our plan was to hire a driver to take us across into Jordan over the Hussein Bridge and checkpoint which is up north, east of Beit She'an, and south of the Galilee. The idea was to travel through the mountains in Jordan and then down to Amman. Our return plan was to go south to the Allenby Bridge and checkpoint near Jericho and reenter Israel and be picked up by our dear friend Ramone. You may remember Ramone. He is the one who keeps me out of trouble and safe in the Middle East as I travel to and fro. Simple plan and it should work, and it did for the most part without any mishaps.

After several hours driving through the hot dessert sun and cooling down somewhat as we were traveling through the mountains we finally arrive in Amman. What a joy to see my son, whom I hadn't seen in many months. He had lost a little weight, his skin looked a little weathered, and had sharpness in his eyes like that of an eagle. The Middle East has a way of effecting people that way. My baby boy was no longer a baby boy; rather, he became a man somewhere along the journey.

We had refreshments and then went on our way to be introduced to the family. What an exercise in faith riding along in a car when someone else is driving through the streets of Amman. Organized chaos is the best way to describe the traffic. To say we were glad to get off the main road would be an understatement.

The Church

We first stopped by the church where he was helping in some of the projects. We met the pastor and his lovely wife and several of the children who were part of this tiny congregation. My heart always breaks for the children who are the ones who suffer the most in any military conflict or social economic crisis. My son was brilliant, loving and with great compassion reflecting the love of Jesus to the people of this poor community in Jordan.

Meeting the Father

Next we traveled through the winding streets, alleyways leaving the trash filled streets with burning barrels of fire to a more pristine part of town. We pulled up on a nice driveway and there before us was a beautiful home with a patio veranda around back. My son introduced me and my colleague to the father first and then to the rest of the family.

Introductions

I found it interesting when my son introduced me and my friend, (oh by the way, I never mentioned my colleague is a bible teacher in a Christian High School), the response was Ohhh! or Hmm! I asked my son, "What did you say to them?" He said, "Dad I introduced you as a "Holy Man" because you are a minister, and I introduced Chuck, (my colleague) as "One who studies holy books" because he is a Christian school teacher." My son was now validated! He is known in that family and community as "Scott, son of the holy man Jeff." That evening the men sat in one part of the house and the daughters served their father, the "holy man" and "the one who studies holy books." Then came time for the photo. The father sat on a chair, I sat on one side and Chuck on the other and the rest of the family and friends stood behind the patriarch and the honored guests.

The family with Dr. Jeff, Scott and friend Chuck.

My son now has an open door to return to this family. The father, by his actions and the words that he spoke honored me by welcoming me into his home any time. His actions matched his words.

My Son's Sanctuary

Now the mission accomplished it was time for Chuck and me to travel back home to Israel. Before heading back to Israel we had to sleep as it was late in the evening. We stayed in my son's apartment. Walking through dark narrow streets, dogs barking, cats meowing, passing trash cans, through the metal gate, up the stone stairs in the yard of dirt, to a stone building with bars across the windows with the smell of cat urine, we stepped across the threshold into this sanctuary of safety, peace and love. We showered and cleaned up from our day. Sitting upon mattresses on the floor with a dim light bulb hanging from a wire over head the three of us prayed, read scripture and thanked the Lord for a marvelous day. In the distanced you could hear the Muslim clerics sing their prayers echoing through the valleys.

As our heads hit our perspective moldy pillows our eyes closed and we went fast to sleep. Roosters and sounds of cats in the garbage woke us the next morning. It was time to travel back literally crossing the Jordan River into the land of Abraham, Isaac and Jacob.

Saying Goodbye

We said our goodbyes. Leaving your children is never an easy thing to do. My eyes filled with tears as our driver started his car and Chuck and I climbed in and down the road we went.

Finally, we came to the Allenby Bridge and checkpoint near Jericho. Everything went fine until I discovered my bag was stolen. We made it through the checkpoint and now we are on the Israeli side. Still no bag… it was obviously stolen on the Jordanian side of security. It was my own foolish mistake. Usually I keep my bag with me, but for some reason, (we were pretty exhausted), I let it go through security without it being attached to my right arm.

"Follow us!"

I approached several Israeli soldiers and shared my plight with them. With swiftness and determination, they said, "Follow us!" I did. They escorted me back over to the Jordanian side of the checkpoint, and we walked into the inner most part of Jordanian security looking for my bag. It was like the parting of the Red Sea. The Jordanian security moved aside as they saw this 6 foot two inch American and a band of Israeli soldiers. It was quite impressive and intimidating at the same time. Didn't find the bag. It was long gone. Lesson learned…hold on to your bags.

Loyal Friend

The whole process took about three hours. Meanwhile, Ramone, our dear friend who was to pick us up stood outside by his car in the 115 degree heat of the Judean wilderness. We told him we would be there at a certain time. The time had come and gone. He was aggressively inquiring as to our safety and whereabouts. He was running out of water, and yet he stayed there until we came through the gates of the checkpoint.

Ramone is the type of man that would have waited for us throughout the night. Why? Because we said we would be there, and as friends, we have proven that our words match our actions. We have blessed his family and he has blessed ours. When we finally walked through the gates and saw his profusely dehydrated body standing near the car we were delighted to say the least. His arms were waving and he was shouting, "Baruch HaShem!" Praise the Lord. He said over and over, Praise the Lord, you are alright my brother!" We hugged his sweat-soaked body, he kissed us on the cheeks, and we piled into the car. Up to Jerusalem we would go. What a joy it was to be back home driving up the Judean mountains, through the Mount of Olives, Mount Zion and finally arriving in Moriah the main mountain of Jerusalem.

Principles to Remember:

1. *A father will respond to his son's request*. So it is that our Heavenly Father will respond to His children when they call to Him (Matthew 7:7-11).

2. *What you do is who you are*. You can say good words, and good words are necessary, however, it is your actions that measure you. You are known by what you do. (Proverbs 22:1; James 1:21-27; 2:14-20)

3. *With friendship loyalty is important*. A true friend will lay down his life for another. Believers have a true friend that is closer than a brother (John 15:13,14; Proverbs 18:24).

4. *There is joy in coming home*. No matter how far you've traveled, there is joy in coming home. There is peace, love, acceptance and assurance. For the believer, our home is found in Yeshua the Messiah. Daily, you can walk with Him and talk with Him. Where Jesus is there you will find the Christian's home. One day we will rule and reign with Jesus 1,000 years where His throne will be in Jerusalem. We will also spend eternity with Him throughout the ages to come. Those who believe in Jesus truly do find purpose and peace.

(Deuteronomy 28:13; Isaiah 2; Ezekiel 40-48; Matthew 25; John 14; Colossians 1; Revelation 20-22).

Louise and I thank you for your prayers, encouragement and support along the way! Pray for the peace of Jerusalem. Bless God's ancient people and you will be blessed!

Chapter 5
Mountain of Great Joy!

Prelude

Two years before our great journey, Louise and I committed ourselves to prayer. We sought counsel from godly men, stayed on our knees seeking the face of God, crying out to Him for clear direction. The way we were to go progressively became clear as God began to open doors and confirm His desire for us. With great circumspection we took our first step, then second, third, fourth…

The Mountain

What was before us was like a beautiful mountain overlooking a valley and coastline. The mountain was like a monument standing in majestic glory for all to see. This mountain was a mountain of great joy to the Lord. To climb this mountain would take faith, a lot of faith. To ascend would also take much courage and strength that would be beyond our measure, or ability to achieve alone. We would need help from above, and from friends, loved ones and those who would personally embrace our vision and love for the seed of Abraham.

The Valley

The lush valley had a river springing forth from the mountain with thousands of diverse and beautiful flowers and fruit trees dotting the hilly terrain. The fruited valley was like a place of hope for all to enjoy. To work the ground, and nurture the life that was growing throughout would take divine intervention and a multitude of volunteers who would daily commit themselves to prayer, lending a hand to Louise and me as we journeyed into the unknown.

The Coast, The Child, The Call

The coastline was pristine with white sand and palms, a gateway to the world. In the shadow of the palms stood a child, weakened with hunger unable to climb the trees for food. The child looked for someone to help. Tears were flowing from the child's eyes. Danger lurked on every side. The child was vulnerable. "Lord, who will help this little one?" "It is written, *'Inasmuch as ye have done it unto one of the lest of these my brethren, ye have done it unto me.'* –(Jesus, Matthew 25:40)"

"What do you mean Lord? What do you want us to do?" *"I want you to touch my chosen people and the seed of Abraham, 'for he that touches (Israel) touches the apple of (my) eye' (Zechariah 2:8)."*

"Lord, how will we bless your people, for we have little to offer, no resources, no money, people won't listen? How can we do this thing you ask?" *"I will bless them that bless Israel (Genesis 12:3)."*

"Lord, specifically, how do you want us to bless Israel and Abraham's seed?" *"If the Gentiles have been made partakers of their spiritual things (Jewish roots), their (the Gentile's) duty is to minister unto them (the Jews) in material things (Romans 15:27)."*

One in Three

To meet the physical needs of 30% of Israel's children who are impoverished is a big task that requires prayer and financial help from many people. According to a survey by Israel's Health Ministry the number of malnourished Jewish children was 13.5%. Among the Arab population one in three children is poverty-stricken to the point of malnutrition.
– Gil Horev, www.maarivintl.com, November 1, 2004

Willing to Go

"Did you see a vision Jeff?" "No." However, that which God has called Louise and me to do is like this mountain, valley, coastline and child. There is food and hope available for this child. But who is willing to go and respond? We are!

Therefore, Louise and I did the only thing we could do. Respond to God in faith. In August 2002 I resigned my church, and we stepped out in faith trusting God for every need as we created a new ministry.

Your prayers and donations help feed this child. This child represents the 30% of the children who need our help.

Bringing Hope

When you pray for us, you are bringing hope to this solitary needy child.

When you give a donation, you are bringing life to this malnourished child.

When you pray, and give a donation you are enabling us to teach the Word of God, encourage Christians, proclaim the gospel and feed those in need.

When you pray and give a donation, you climb the mountain with us, you plow the ground with us, you pluck the fruit with us, and present it to the child, and from this child, to the world.

Miracles:

1. Thousands given a meal

2. Speaking engagements throughout the US and Middle East to thousands of people

3. Radio programs and interviews throughout the US:

4. Recording Equipment

5. Apartments made available to us while staying in Israel

6. Growing network in the Middle East among Jews and Arabs, believers and non-believers

7. Safety while traveling throughout villages, cities and towns in the Middle East, and the U.S.

8. Obtained needed office equipment

9. Faithful prayer and financial supporters

10. Monthly teaching and ministry updates; plus, several published books

These are a few of the miracles God has fashioned for Louise and me. Allow me to share with you a few prayer requests:

Prayer:

1. Continued growth in reaching Jews and Arabs with a meal and the gospel

2. Office space and ministry location where we can maximize ITM's resources

3. Blessing upon Speaking engagements, radio and teaching literature

4. Continued growth in number of monthly prayer and financial supporters

5. Safety as we travel

Scripture is certainly right when it says that in the latter days men will be lovers of self and preoccupied with false peace (2 Timothy 3:1-5). This is very evident. Need we fear? No. The Word teaches us that God is faithful and even though the mountains may fall into the sea, He remains in control of His world (Psalm 46:1-2).

Your prayers, encouragement and financial support have enabled us to keep going in these dark and violent times. To be honest, it is not easy. We face pressures on every side but knowing that our ITM family is behind us makes the load lighter. A letter and update like this could never adequately express our gratitude to you. So, know that with these "feeble words" comes a humble heart full of gratitude and appreciation.

Your generous financial support is as a light shining in very dark places! You have no idea the encouragement we receive from your support. Our arms are strengthened as we are able to carry out this timely and strategic ministry. Thank you!